Table

Introduction

Finnish Breakfast Recipes

   Mushrooms Omelet Roll

   Breakfast Pasties

   Oven Cooked Cheese Breakfast

   Lingonberry Porridge

   Meat Pasties

   Scandinavian Crab Cakes

   Potato Flatbread

   Easy Breakfast Rice Pies

   Fast Potatoes and Eggs

   Baked Pancake

Finnish Salad Recipes

   Easy Rosolli Salad

   Great Mushrooms Salad

   Finnish Seafood Salad

   Ham Salad

   Potato Salad

   Tuna Salad

   Herring Salad

   Crab Salad

   Balsamic Potato Salad

- Finnish Cucumber Salad
- Finnish Soup Recipes
  - Salmon Soup
  - Chanterelle Soup
  - Delicious Green Pea Soup
  - Easy Crayfish Soup
  - Spinach Soup
  - Veggie Soup
  - Pike Soup
  - Broccoli Soup
  - Delicious Trout Soup
  - Special Garlic Soup
- Finnish Main Dish Recipes
  - Great Beef Stew
  - Stuffed Cabbage
  - Finnish Hot Meat Stew
  - Lamb Roast
  - Cabbage and Tofu Mix
  - Herbed Salmon
  - Finnish Beef Mix
  - Reindeer Stew
  - Stuffed Peppers
  - Creamy Rutabaga Bake
  - Fish Dinner Mix

- Roasted Salmon
- Pork and Beef Meatballs
- Tasty Beef Steaks
- Flavored Chicken Mix
- Trout and Spinach
- Fish Pudding
- Smoked Mackerel Mix
- Smoked Salmon Bowls
- Ceviche

Finnish Dessert Recipes

- Simple Rice Fritters
- Finnish Cookies
- Tasty Round Cookies
- Great Cranberry Cream
- Blueberry Pie
- Plums Stew
- Rhubarb Puddings
- Red Currant Smoothie
- Rich Rice Pudding
- Apple Pie

Conclusion

Author's Afterthoughts

Introduction

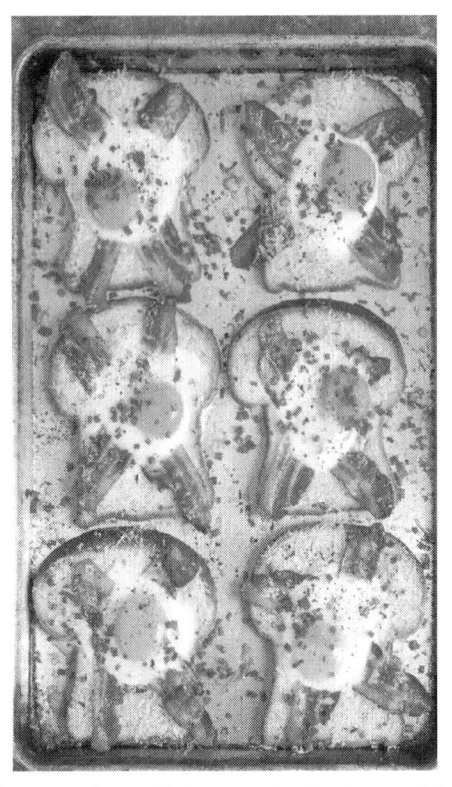

Finland is one of the most beautiful countries in the world. It will amaze you with its landscapes, villages, towns and welcoming local people. Once you understand how magical this country is you will love it for sure!

This brings us to what we really want you to discover today!

One more aspect you will end up loving about Finland is its cuisine. All Finns are extremely passionate about their food and their recipes. They celebrate a wide variety of foods, flavors and textures and they have a huge respect for their culinary roots. Let's be honest! You can't find this anywhere!

Finns love their local ingredients, their original and traditional dishes and maybe that's why Finnish food tastes so great!

Are you curious to discover whey Finns love their cuisine? Then, this is the right place for you! We were as curious as you to learn about the Finnish cuisine and that's why we developed this unbelievable Finnish recipe collection! We gathered the best breakfast ideas, salads, soups, main dishes and desserts and we want to share them all with you! It is really a fascinating world full of textures, richness and taste! It's a magical culinary journey you will remember! So, are you ready to start this culinary trip? Are you ready to discover Finland's feasts? Then let's get started! Enjoy Finland and its cuisine as much as we did!

Have fun!

Finnish Breakfast Recipes

A traditional Finnish day begins with a rich and tasty breakfast recipe. Therefore, we gathered the best ones for you to try as soon as possible!

Mushrooms Omelet Roll

It looks so delicious but it tastes even better!

Preparation time: 10 minutes
Cooking time: 20 minutes
Servings: 6
Ingredients:

- 6 eggs, whisked
- 1 cup milk
- 2 tablespoons flour
- A pinch of salt and black pepper
- 3 tablespoons olive oil
- 1 pound mushrooms, chopped
- 2 onions, chopped
- 1 tablespoon basil, chopped

Method:
1. In a bowl, mix the eggs with the milk, flour, salt and pepper and whisk well.
2. Heat up a pan with 1 tablespoon olive oil over medium high heat, add the eggs mixture, spread into the pan, cook for 3 minutes, flip, cook for another 3 minutes and transfer to a plate.
3. Heat up the same pan with the rest of the oil over medium high heat, add the onions, stir and sauté for 3 minutes.
4. Add the mushrooms, stir and cook for 5 minutes more.
5. Spread this mixture over the omelet, sprinkle basil, roll the omelet, place it in a greased baking dish, introduce in the oven at 390 degrees F for 5 minutes, slice and serve for breakfast.

Enjoy!

Breakfast Pasties

Extremely tasty and very rich breakfast idea!

Preparation time: 10 minutes
Cooking time: 45 minutes
Servings: 8
Ingredients:

- 4 and ½ cups white flour
- 1 cup olive oil
- A pinch of salt and black pepper
- 1 and ¼ cups cold water
- 5 and ½ cups potatoes, peeled and diced
- 2 carrots, shredded
- 1 yellow onion, chopped
- ½ cup rutabaga, chopped

- 1 and ½ pounds beef, ground
- ½ pound pork, ground
- 1 beef bouillon cube, dissolved in hot water

Method:
1. In a bowl, mix the flour with the oil, salt, pepper and water and stir until you obtain a dough.
2. In a separate bowl, mix the potatoes with the carrots, onion, rutabaga, beef, pork and bouillon cube and stir well.
3. Roll the dough on a working surface, divide it into squares, divide the stuffing in the center of each, fold and seal edges and arrange them all on a lined baking sheet.
4. Introduce in the oven, bake at 425 degrees F for 45 minutes, divide between plates and serve for breakfast.

Enjoy!

Oven Cooked Cheese Breakfast

This breakfast idea will fascinate your loved ones for sure!

Preparation time: 10 minutes

Cooking time: 25 minutes

Servings: 6

Ingredients:

- 2 and ½ gallons milk
- A pinch of salt
- 1 tablespoon cornstarch
- 1 tablespoon sugar
- ½ tablet Hanson's rennet

Method:

1. Put the milk in a double boiler and heat it up over 88 degrees F.
2. In a cup, mix the salt with cornstarch and sugar and stir.
3. Add some of the milk, and the crushed tablet, whisk well and pour over the milk.
4. Stir and set aside for 45 minutes.
5. Pour the jelled mixture into a cake pan in which you arranged a wet cloth.
6. Gather the corners of the cloth, take it out of the pan and squeeze the liquid as much as possible.
7. Remove the cloth, press the cheese in the pan, introduce in the oven and bake at 400 degrees F for 15 minutes.
8. Cool the cheese down and serve it for breakfast.

Enjoy!

Lingonberry Porridge

It's a cold but delicious porridge will be an instant hit!
Preparation time: 10 minutes
Cooking time: 25 minutes
Servings: 4
Ingredients:
- 3 cups water
- 1 cup lingonberries, mashed
- 3 tablespoons sugar
- 1 cup semolina

Method:
1. Put the water in a pot, bring to a boil over medium heat, add mashed lingonberries and sugar, stir, cook for 10 minutes and

strain the cooking liquid into a clean pot.
2. Add the semolina, bring to a boil again over low heat and cook for 15 minutes more.
3. Cool the porridge down completely, whisk it well, divide into bowls and serve cold for breakfast.

Enjoy!

Meat Pasties

This is so fulfilling and delightful!

Preparation time: 10 minutes

Cooking time: 20 minutes

Servings: 4

Ingredients:

- 1 and ½ cups flour
- 1 cup milk
- ½ tablespoons yeast
- ½ tablespoon sugar
- 1 pound beef, ground
- 1 yellow onion, chopped
- 4 tablespoons white rice
- A pinch of salt and white pepper
- ¼ cup sour cream
- 1 egg, whisked

- Oil for frying, a drizzle

Method:
1. In a bowl, mix the flour with the milk, sugar and yeast, stir well, shape a dough out of this mix and leave aside to rise.
2. Heat up a pan with a drizzle of oil over medium high heat, add the onion, stir and cook for 2-3 minutes.
3. Add the rice, the beef, salt, pepper and sour cream, stir, brown for 5 minutes more and take off the heat.
4. Divide the dough into medium balls, flatten each, divide the meat mixture equally into the center of each flattened dough ball dough's Fold the dough over the meat and seal the edges, making sure to brush all the pasties with egg wash.
5. Heat up a pan with a drizzle of oil over medium high heat, add the pasties, cook them until they are golden on both sides, drain excess grease on paper towels, divide between plates and serve for breakfast.

Enjoy!

Scandinavian Crab Cakes

It's easy to make these crab cakes and they taste so good!

Preparation time: 10 minutes

Cooking time: 10 minutes

Servings: 6

Ingredients:

- 1 egg, whisked
- ¼ teaspoon curry powder
- 1 tablespoon homemade mayonnaise
- 3 drops hot pepper sauce

- 1 teaspoon Worcestershire sauce
- 1 tablespoon lemon juice
- A pinch of cayenne pepper
- ½ teaspoon paprika
- 1 pound crabmeat
- ¼ teaspoon mustard seeds, ground
- 1 tablespoon lemon pepper
- 5 tablespoons bread crumbs
- 5 tablespoon olive oil

Method:

1. In a bowl, combine the crab meat with the egg, curry powder, mayonnaise, pepper sauce, Worcestershire sauce, lemon juice, cayenne, paprika, mustard seeds, lemon pepper and bread crumbs, stir well and shape medium cakes out of this mix.
2. Heat up a pan with the oil over medium to high heat, add the crab cakes, cook them for 5-6 minutes on each side, divide between plates and serve for breakfast.

Enjoy!

Potato Flatbread

This is a very easy and tasty breakfast idea for you to try!

Preparation time: 10 minutes
Cooking time: 15 minutes
Servings: 4
Ingredients:

- 1 and ½ cups potato, boiled, peeled and mashed
- ¾ cup barley flour
- 1 egg, whisked

- A pinch of salt
- Butter for serving

Method:
1. In a bowl, combine mashed potato with the flour, egg and salt and stir well until you obtain a dough.
2. Transfer the dough to a floured working surface, flatten it and divide into 4 servings.
3. Shape your disks, arrange them all on a lined baking sheet, prick them with a fork, place into the oven and bake at 428 degrees F for 15 minutes.
4. Divide the breads between plates, spread the butter over them and serve for breakfast.

Enjoy!

Easy Breakfast Rice Pies

You'll be impressed with the taste! We are sure!

Preparation time: 10 minutes

Cooking time: 55 minutes

Servings: 4

Ingredients:

- 1 cup white rice
- 1 cup rye flour
- ¼ cup white flour
- A pinch of salt
- 2 cups milk
- 3 tablespoons butter, melted

- 2 and ½ cup water

Method:
1. Put 2 cups water in a pan, add the rice, bring to a boil over medium heat, cover and cook for 20 minutes.
2. Add the milk and salt, stir well and cook for 20 minutes more.
3. In a bowl, mix the rye flour with the white one and ½ cup water and stir until you have a sticky dough consistency.
4. Transfer the dough to a floured working surface, divide into 16 servings and roll each piece into a circle.
5. Divide the rice mixture in the center of the circles, spread almost until the edges, fold the edges and crimp them shaping small boats.
6. Arrange all the pies on a lined baking sheet, introduce in the oven and bake at 450 degrees F for 15 minutes.
7. Serve them for breakfast.

Enjoy!

Fast Potatoes and Eggs

It's an amazing breakfast combination!
Preparation time: 10 minutes
Cooking time: 10 minutes
Servings: 6
Ingredients:

- 6 bacon slices, cooked and crumbled
- 8 potatoes, boiled, peeled and diced
- 1 yellow onion, chopped
- 2 tablespoons butter
- 2 cups lamb, cooked and shredded
- 6 eggs, fried

Method:

1. Heat up a pan with the butter over medium high heat, add the onion, stir and sauté for 5 minutes.
2. Add the potatoes and the lamb meat, stir and cook for 5 minutes more.
3. Divide the potato hash between plates, top each serving with a fried egg, sprinkle the crumbled bacon on top and serve for breakfast.

    Enjoy!

Baked Pancake

This is a very interesting breakfast idea!

Preparation time: 10 minutes
Cooking time: 15 minutes
Servings: 4
Ingredients:

- 6 eggs
- 1 and ½ cups milk
- ¼ cup sugar
- 1 tablespoon vanilla sugar
- ½ teaspoon lemon zest, grated
- 1 and ½ cups flour
- 1 teaspoon baking powder

- 1/3 cup butter, melted

Method:
1. In a bowl, mix the eggs with the milk, sugar, vanilla sugar, lemon zest, flour, baking powder and butter and stir well.
2. Pour the batter in a round baking dish, introduce in the oven and bake at 450 degrees F for 15 minutes.
3. Slice the pancakes, divide it between plates and serve for breakfast.

Enjoy!

Finnish Salad Recipes

Finnish salads are rich, delicious and they look incredible! We searched and gathered the best salad recipes for you to try! Check out how to prepare them for your loved ones!

Easy Rosolli Salad

It's incredibly easy to make and it tastes just amazing!

Preparation time: 10 minutes
Cooking time: 0 minutes
Servings: 4
Ingredients:

- 4 potatoes, boiled, peeled and cubed
- 4 carrots, boiled, peeled and cubed
- 4 pickled beetroot, peeled and cubed
- 1 yellow onion, chopped
- A pinch of salt and white pepper

- 1 and ½ cup sour cream
- 1 and ½ teaspoon vinegar
- 1 and ½ teaspoon sugar

Method:

1. In a salad bowl, mix the potatoes with the carrots, beetroot, onion, salt, pepper, sour cream, vinegar and sugar, toss well and serve.

Enjoy!

Great Mushrooms Salad

The taste is simply wonderful!
Preparation time: 10 minutes
Cooking time: 0 minutes
Servings: 4
Ingredients:
- 1 pound salted mushrooms, soaked for several hours, drained well and sliced
- 1 yellow onion, diced
- 1 cup sour cream
- 2 teaspoons lemon juice
- ½ teaspoon sugar

- A pinch of white pepper

Method:
1. In a salad bowl, mix the mushrooms with the onion, sour cream, lemon juice, sugar and pepper, toss well, divide into smaller bowls and serve cold.

   Enjoy!

Finnish Seafood Salad

It's so fresh and so tasty! It's just perfect!

Preparation time: 10 minutes
Cooking time: 3 minutes
Servings: 8
Ingredients:

- 4 pounds big shrimp
- 3 tablespoons salt
- 1 tablespoon lemon juice
- 2 cups mayonnaise
- 1 teaspoon mustard
- 2 tablespoons white vinegar
- A pinch of black pepper
- 6 tablespoons dill, chopped
- 1 cup red onion, chopped

- 3 cups celery, minced

Method:
1. Put enough water in a pot and bring to a simmer over medium heat.
2. Add the salt and the shrimp, stir, boil for 3 minutes, drain, peel and devein the shrimp.
3. In a salad bowl, combine the shrimp with mayonnaise, mustard, vinegar, lemon juice, black pepper, dill, onion and celery and toss.
4. Serve the salad cold.

    Enjoy!

Ham Salad

This is a traditional Finnish salad you can serve with a Sunday meal!
Preparation time: 10 minutes
Cooking time: 0 minutes
Servings: 4

Ingredients:

- 1 cucumber, sliced
- 1 cup kilta cheese, grated
- 1 cup favorite cheese, grated
- 2 pickles, chopped
- 4 apples, cored, peeled and cubed
- 4 tomatoes, chopped
- 2 cups macaroni, boiled and drained
- 1 cup sour cream
- 1 and ½ tablespoons lemon juice
- 1 and ½ tablespoons mustard
- 1 tablespoon sugar
- 1 tablespoon parsley, chopped
- A pinch of black pepper

Method:

1. In a large salad bowl, combine the cucumber with kilta cheese, favorite cheese, pickles, apples, tomatoes and macaroni.
2. Add sour cream, lemon juice, mustard, sugar, parsley and black pepper, toss and serve cold.

    Enjoy!

Potato Salad

You can make this today! Everyone will love it!

Preparation time: 10 minutes

Cooking time: 20 minutes

Servings: 5

Ingredients:

- 3 pounds potatoes, peeled and halved
- 2 cups mayonnaise
- ½ cup mustard
- ½ cup red vinegar
- 4 scallions, chopped
- 1 carrot, shredded
- 1 celery rib, shredded

- A pinch of salt and black pepper
- ¼ cup parsley, chopped

Method:
1. Put the potatoes in a pot, add water to cover, bring to a boil over medium high heat, cook for 20 minutes, drain and cut into cubes.
2. In a salad bowl, mix the potatoes with the mayonnaise, mustard, vinegar, scallions, carrot, celery, salt, pepper and parsley, toss and serve cold.

    Enjoy!

Tuna Salad

It's the perfect tuna dish for a summers day!

Preparation time: 10 minutes
Cooking time: 0 minutes
Servings: 4
Ingredients:

- 1 cup already cooked rice
- 1 cup tuna, shredded
- 6 ounces peas, cooked
- ½ leek, chopped
- ½ cucumber, sliced
- 1 green apple, cored, peeled and cubed

- Juice of ½ lemon
- A handful dill, chopped
- 1 garlic clove, minced
- 2/3 cup sour cream
- 1 teaspoon ketchup
- A pinch of black pepper

Method:

1. In a salad bowl, mix the rice with tuna, peas, leek, cucumber, apple, lemon juice and dill and toss.
2. Add the garlic, sour cream, ketchup and black pepper, toss and serve.

Enjoy!

Herring Salad

Your favorite fish salad is here!

Preparation time: 2 hours and 10 minutes
Cooking time: 1 hour
Servings: 4
Ingredients:

- 8 ounces beets
- A pinch of salt and black pepper
- 2 cups water
- 1 cup sugar
- 1 tablespoons allspice
- 4 bay leaves
- ½ tablespoon white peppercorns
- 1 cinnamon stick
- 1 tablespoon cloves

- 1 red onion, chopped
- 1 green apple, cored, peeled and chopped
- 4 ounces potatoes, boiled and cubed
- 4 ounces pickled herring, shredded
- 1/3 cup sour cream
- ¼ cup chives, chopped
- ¼ cup dill, chopped
- A pinch of salt and black pepper

Method:
1. Wrap the beets in tin foil, arrange them on a lined baking sheet, introduce in the oven at 375 degrees F, bake for 1 hour, peel and cube them.
2. In a bowl, mix the water with the sugar, allspice, bay leaves, peppercorns, cinnamon and cloves and whisk well.
3. Add the beets, onion and the apple, leave aside for 2 hours, strain well and transfer to a salad bowl.
4. Add boiled potatoes, pickled herring, sour cream, chives, dill, salt and pepper, toss and serve cold.

   Enjoy!

Crab Salad

This is a very simple salad to prepare for your family !

Preparation time: 10 minutes
Cooking time: 0 minutes
Servings: 4
Ingredients:

- 8 ounces canned jumbo crab meat
- 8 ounces canned special crab meat
- 1 shallot, minced
- 2 celery ribs, chopped
- ½ cup red bell pepper, chopped
- 2 tablespoons lime juice
- 2 tablespoons parsley, chopped

- ½ teaspoon bay seasoning
- ½ teaspoon garlic powder
- A pinch of salt and black pepper
- ½ cup mayonnaise

Method:
1. In a salad bowl, combine the crab meat with the shallot, celery, bell pepper, lime juice, parsley, bay seasoning, garlic powder, salt, pepper and mayonnaise.
2. Toss and serve the salad cold.

Enjoy!

Balsamic Potato Salad

This potato salad is so yummy!

Preparation time: 10 minutes

Cooking time: 20 minutes

Servings: 4

Ingredients:

- 2 pounds potatoes
- A pinch of salt and black pepper
- 2 tablespoons mustard
- 3 tablespoons olive oil
- 2 tablespoons balsamic vinegar
- 1 tablespoon chives, chopped

Method:

1. Put the potatoes in a pot, add water to cover, bring to a boil over

medium heat, cook for 20 minutes, drain, peel and cut them into cubes.
2. In a salad bowl, mix the potatoes with salt, pepper, mustard, oil, vinegar and chives, toss and serve.

Enjoy!

Finnish Cucumber Salad

It's a perfect summer salad!
Preparation time: 10 minutes
Cooking time: 0 minutes
Servings: 4
Ingredients:

- 3 cucumbers, thinly sliced
- 1/3 cup cider vinegar
- ¼ cup water
- 2 tablespoons olive oil

- 4 tablespoons sugar
- A pinch of salt and black pepper
- 1 tablespoon dill, chopped

Method:

1. In a salad bowl, mix the cucumbers with the vinegar, water, oil, sugar, salt, pepper and dill, toss and serve cold.

Enjoy!

Finnish Soup Recipes

You are about to learn how to make real feasts for your family and friends! You are going to discover the richest and most textured Finnish soups. Check them all out!

Salmon Soup

This marvelous soup will surprise you for sure!

Preparation time: 10 minutes
Cooking time: 35 minutes
Servings: 4
Ingredients:

- 1 pound salmon fillets, skinless, boneless and cubed
- 4 tablespoons butter
- 1 leek, sliced
- 5 cups fish stock
- 1 pound potatoes, peeled and cubed
- 1 carrot, chopped
- 1 cup dill, chopped
- 1 cup heavy cream
- ¼ teaspoon allspice

- A pinch of salt and black pepper

Method:
1. Heat up a pot with the butter over medium heat, add the leeks, stir and cook for 10 minutes.
2. Add the stock, stir and cook for 10 minutes more.
3. Add potatoes, carrots, allspice, salt, pepper and half of the dill, stir and cook for 10 minutes.
4. Add the salmon and the cream, stir and cook for 5 minutes more.
5. Add the rest of the dill, toss, divide the soup into bowls and serve.

Enjoy!

Chanterelle Soup

This is such a creamy soup! You'll see!

Preparation time: 10 minutes
Cooking time: 50 minutes
Servings: 5
Ingredients:

- 6 cups chicken stock
- 6 tablespoons butter
- 2 tablespoons flour
- 1 pound chanterelle mushrooms, sliced
- 2 shallots, chopped
- 3 egg yolks
- ½ cup heavy cream

- ¼ teaspoon saffron powder
- A pinch of salt and black pepper

Method:
1. Heat up a pot with 2 tablespoons butter over medium high heat, add the flour and stir well.
2. Add the stock, whisk well and cook for 20 minutes.
3. Heat up another pot with the rest of the butter over medium high heat, add the shallots, stir and cook for 5 minutes.
4. Add the mushrooms, stir and cook for 5 minutes more.
5. Add the stock, stir, bring to a boil, cook for 10 minutes and blend using an immersion blender.
6. In a bowl, mix the cream with egg yolks, saffron, salt and pepper and whisk well.
7. Add some of the cooking liquid and whisk well again.
8. Pour this into the pot, stir, cook for 10 minutes more, ladle into bowls and serve.

Enjoy!

Delicious Green Pea Soup

Everyone will ask for more! That's how tasty it is!
Preparation time: 10 minutes
Cooking time: 20 minutes
Servings: 4
Ingredients:

- 16 ounces peas
- 1 shallot, chopped
- ½ yellow onion, chopped
- 2 tablespoons olive oil

- 1 cup veggie stock
- 1 and ½ cups water
- A pinch of salt and black pepper
- 1 tablespoon chives, chopped

Method:

1. Heat up a pot with the oil over medium high heat, add the onions, stir and cook for 5 minutes.
2. Add the shallots, stir and cook for 5 minutes more.
3. Add the stock and the water, stir and bring to a boil.
4. Add the peas, stir, cook for 10 minutes and take off the heat.
5. Blend the soup using an immersion blender, divide the soup into bowls and serve with chives sprinkled on top.

   Enjoy!

Easy Crayfish Soup

You will simply adore this great seafood soup!
Preparation time: 10 minutes
Cooking time: 1 hour and 10 minutes
Servings: 4
Ingredients:

- 4 pounds crayfish
- 2 tablespoons canola oil
- ½ cup cognac
- 2 celery stalks, chopped

- 1 carrot, chopped
- 6 garlic cloves, minced
- 2 tablespoons tomato paste
- 7 cups fish stock
- 1 tablespoon thyme, chopped
- 3 bay leaves
- 1 and ½ teaspoon arrowroot powder
- 1 cup crème fraiche
- A pinch of salt and black pepper
- 2 tablespoons chives, chopped

Method:
1. Put some water in a pot, bring to a boil over high heat, add crayfish, cook for 5 minutes, drain and rinse.
2. Peel and devein the crayfish and put the meat in a bowl.
3. Heat up a pot with the oil over medium high heat, add crayfish shells and cook for 3 minutes.
4. Add the cognac, lightly ignite it for a few seconds and leave the flame to die.
5. Reduce heat to low, add celery, garlic and carrots, stir and cook for 15 minutes more.
6. Add tomato paste, stock, thyme and bay leaves, stir and cook for 30 minutes.
7. Strain the soup into another pot, discard shells, veggies and the herbs and simmer the soup over medium heat for 20 minutes more.
8. In a bowl, mix the arrowroot powder with 2 tablespoons soup, whisk well and pour into the pot.
9. Also add salt, pepper, crayfish meat and crème fraiche, cook everything for 2 minutes more, ladle the soup into bowls, sprinkle the chives on top and serve.

Enjoy!

Spinach Soup

This will become one of your favorite soups!

Preparation time: 10 minutes
Cooking time: 12 minutes
Servings: 4
Ingredients:

- 3 tablespoons butter, melted
- 5 tablespoons flour
- 5 cups milk
- 3 ounces spinach, chopped
- A pinch of salt and white pepper
- 1 teaspoon sugar
- 4 eggs, hard boiled, peeled and halved

Method:

1. Heat up a pot with the butter over medium high heat, add the flour and whisk well.
2. Add half of the milk, whisk well and bring to a boil.
3. Add the rest of the milk, the spinach, salt and pepper, whisk and simmer over medium heat for 10 minutes.

4. Add sugar, stir, cook for 2 minutes, more, divide into bowls and top each serving with 2 egg halves.

Enjoy!

Veggie Soup

It's a simple, yet so delicious summer soup!
Preparation time: 10 minutes
Cooking time: 20 minutes
Servings: 4
Ingredients:
- 5 cups water
- 2 tablespoons sugar
- A pinch of salt and black pepper

- 3 carrots, peeled and sliced
- 1 cauliflower, florets separated
- 5 potatoes, peeled and diced
- A handful pea pods
- 3 radishes, chopped
- A handful spinach, torn
- 1 cup milk
- 3 tablespoons flour
- 2 tablespoons butter

Method:

1. Put the water in a pot and bring to a simmer over medium heat.
2. Add the carrots, cauliflower, potatoes, pea pods, radishes, salt, pepper and the sugar, stir and simmer for 15 minutes.
3. Add the spinach, stir and cook for 2 minutes more.
4. In a bowl, mix the milk with the flour, whisk well and add to the pot.
5. Also add the butter, whisk, simmer for 3 minutes more, ladle the soup into bowls and serve.

Enjoy!

Pike Soup

This is so textured and tasty!
Preparation time: 10 minutes
Cooking time: 25 minutes
Servings: 5
Ingredients:

- 5 cups fish stock
- 1 yellow onion, chopped
- 5 allspice berries
- A pinch of salt and black pepper
- 5 potatoes, peeled and cubed
- 1 pound pike fillets, boneless and cubed
- 1 tablespoon chives, chopped
- 1 tablespoon dill, chopped

- 1 tablespoon parsley, chopped

Method:
1. Put the stock in a pot, bring to a boil over medium heat, add the onion, potatoes, some salt and pepper, stir and cook for 10 minutes.
2. Add berries, stir and cook for 10 minutes more.
3. Add fish cubes and chives, stir, cook for 5 minutes, divide into bowls, sprinkle the dill and parsley on top and serve.

Enjoy!

Broccoli Soup

This cheesy soup is so amazing!
Preparation time: 10 minutes
Cooking time: 30 minutes
Servings: 6
Ingredients:

- 2 cup potatoes, cubed
- 2 cups broccoli florets, chopped

- 1 cup celery, chopped
- 1 yellow onion, chopped
- 2 quarts water
- 3 chicken bouillon cubes
- 6 tablespoons flour
- 6 tablespoons butter
- ¾ cup milk
- 2 cups cheddar, shredded

Method:

1. Put the water in a pot, add potatoes, broccoli, celery, chicken bouillon and the onion, stir, bring to a simmer over medium heat and cook for 20 minutes.
2. Heat up a pan with the butter over medium high heat, add the flour and whisk well.
3. Add the milk, whisk well, cook for 5 minutes and pour over the soup.
4. Whisk the soup, add the cheese, cook for 5 minutes more, divide into bowls and serve.

Enjoy!

Delicious Trout Soup

You simply must try this delicious fish soup!!
Preparation time: 10 minutes
Cooking time: 30 minutes
Servings: 5
Ingredients:
- 2 trout fillets, boneless and cubed

- 4 potatoes, chopped
- ½ cup celery, cubed
- 4 scallions, chopped
- 4 cups water
- 4 cups goat milk
- 4 tablespoons flour
- ¼ cup goat butter, soft
- 3 bay leaves
- ¼ teaspoon thyme, dried
- ½ teaspoon parsley, chopped
- A pinch of salt and black pepper

Method:

1. Put the water in a pot, add potatoes and celery, stir, bring to a boil over medium heat and cook for 10 minutes.
2. Add thyme, bay leaves, salt and pepper and stir.
3. Heat up a pan with the butter over medium heat, add the scallions, stir and cook for 3-4 minutes.
4. Add the milk, whisk well and cook for 5 minutes more.
5. Add this to your soup, stir and cook for 3-4 minutes.
6. Add the fish, stir, cook for another 5 minutes, divide into bowls and serve.

Enjoy!

Special Garlic Soup

We are sure that you've never tried this before!

Preparation time: 10 minutes

Cooking time: 45 minutes

Servings: 6

Ingredients:

- 2 quarts chicken soup
- ½ cup dark beer
- ½ cup apple cider
- 3 garlic heads, cloves peeled
- 1 garlic head, roasted and pulp squeezed
- 3 potatoes, peeled and cubed
- 2 and ½ tablespoons thyme, chopped
- A pinch of salt and black pepper

- 3 cloves, ground
- 2 bay leaves
- 6 parsley springs
- A pinch of nutmeg powder
- 2 tablespoons bacon fat
- 1 egg yolk
- 2 tablespoons olive oil
- Rye croutons for serving

Method:
1. Put the stock in a pot and heat up over medium heat.
2. Add beer, cider, garlic, roasted garlic, potatoes, cloves, thyme, salt, pepper, nutmeg, bay leaves, bacon fat and parsley springs, stir, bring to a simmer and cook for 45 minutes.
3. Discard bay leaves, blend the soup using an immersion blender and heat up for 1 minute more.
4. In a bowl, whisk the egg yolk with the oil and divide into bowls.
5. Ladle the soup over the egg yolk mixture, top and rye croutons and serve.

Enjoy!

Finnish Main Dish Recipes

Amaze everyone with your cooking skills! Make the best Finnish main dishes for all your guests and loved ones! Try all the recipes we suggest to you today!

Great Beef Stew

A mouthwatering, hearty soup made with a tasty combination of traditional ingredients!!

Preparation time: 10 minutes

Cooking time: 2 hours and 10 minutes

Servings: 6

Ingredients:

- 1 pound beef sirloin, cubed
- 1 tablespoon olive oil
- 1 tablespoon butter
- A pinch of salt and black pepper
- 2 yellow onions, chopped
- 1 teaspoon sugar
- 2 pounds potatoes, peeled and sliced
- 2 cups beer
- 2 cups beef stock

- 1 tablespoon thyme, chopped

Method:
1. Grease a baking dish with the butter and layer the potato slices on the bottom.
2. Heat up a pan with the oil over medium high heat, add the beef, toss, brown for 5 minutes and transfer over the potatoes.
3. Heat up the pan again over medium high heat, add the onions, stir and cook for 2 minutes.
4. Add the sugar, stir, cook for 3 minutes more and transfer over the meat in the baking dish.
5. Add beer, stock, salt and pepper, introduce the dish in the oven and cook the stew at 360 degrees F for 2 hours.
6. Divide the stew into bowls, sprinkle the thyme on top and serve.

Enjoy!

Stuffed Cabbage

Even your most pretentious guests will love this dish!
Preparation time: 10 minutes
Cooking time: 1 hour and 10 minutes
Servings: 5
Ingredients:
- 1 cabbage head, leaves steamed and separated
- 1 pound pork, minced
- 1 yellow onion, chopped
- 4 cups veggie stock
- 2 cups cabbage, chopped

- 1 cup rice, cooked
- A pinch of salt and black pepper
- 1 teaspoon marjoram, dried
- 2 tablespoons butter
- 1 tablespoon flour
- 1 tablespoon cream

Method:

1. Heat up a pan with 2 teaspoons butter over medium high heat, add the onion and cook for 2 minutes.
2. Add the pork, rice, salt, pepper and marjoram, stir, cook for 4-5 minutes and take off the heat.
3. Arrange the cabbage leaves on a working surface, divide the pork mixture, roll and seal edges.
4. Arrange all the rolls in a baking dish and add the stock on top.
5. Heat up a pan with the rest of the butter over medium heat, add the flour and the cream, stir, cook for 2 minutes and pour over the cabbage rolls.
6. Introduce the dish in the oven and bake at 400 degrees F for 1 hour.
7. Divide between plates and serve.

Enjoy!

Finnish Hot Meat Stew

I've got to tell you! This dish really impressed me!

Preparation time: 10 minutes

Cooking time: 8 hours and 10 minutes

Servings: 6

Ingredients:

- 1 pound beef stew meat, cubed
- 1 pound pork stew meat, cubed
- 1 pound lamb stew meat, cubed
- 2 yellow onions, chopped
- 1 tablespoon olive oil
- A pinch of salt and black pepper
- 2 teaspoons peppercorns

- 7 allspice berries
- 2 bay leaves
- 3 cups water

Method:

1. Heat up a pan with the oil over medium high heat, add the onion, stir and cook for 3-4 minutes.
2. Add beef, pork and lamb meat, stir, brown for 5 minutes and transfer everything to your slow cooker.
3. Add peppercorns, allspice, bay leaves and water, toss, cover and cook on Low for 8 hours.
4. Discard bay leaves, divide the stew into bowls and serve.

Enjoy!

Lamb Roast

This dish is so easy to make!
Preparation time: 10 minutes
Cooking time: 1 hour
Servings: 6
Ingredients:

- 1 leg of lamb
- 1 teaspoon dry mustard
- A pinch of salt and black pepper
- 3 garlic cloves, minced
- 1 cup chicken stock

- ½ cup brewed black coffee
- 1 cup cream
- 1 tablespoon flour
- 3 tablespoons red currant jelly, mashed

Method:
1. Make small slits in the lamb leg and rub it with the garlic.
2. Also rub with salt, pepper and dry mustard, place the roast in a baking dish and bake at 450 degrees F for 15 minutes.
3. Reduce heat to 350 degrees F and roast for 15 minutes more.
4. In a bowl, mix the stock with the coffee and half of the cream, whisk well and pour over the lamb.
5. Cook in the oven for 25 minutes more and then leave it aside to rest for a few minutes.
6. Heat up a pan over medium heat, add the flour and stir it for 2 minutes.
7. Add the rest of the cream, salt, pepper and currant jelly, whisk and cook for 5-6 minutes more.
8. Carve the lamb, divide it between plates, spread the sauce all over and serve.

Enjoy!

Cabbage and Tofu Mix

This is the perfect dish to serve your guests!

Preparation time: 10 minutes

Cooking time: 1 hour and 20 minutes

Servings: 6

Ingredients:

For the tofu:

- 1 tablespoon vegetable oil
- 16 ounces tofu, pressed and cubed
- 2 and ½ tablespoons soy sauce
- 2 and ½ tablespoons water
- 1 tablespoon Worcestershire sauce
- ½ teaspoon allspice, ground

For the cabbage:

- 2 tablespoons vegetable oil
- 1 yellow onion, chopped
- 4 cups savoy cabbage, shredded

For the sauce:

- 1 tablespoon white vinegar
- 2 tablespoons tomato paste
- 1 teaspoon dill, dried
- ½ teaspoon sweet paprika
- ¼ cup water
- A pinch of salt and black pepper

Method:

1. In a baking dish, mix the tofu with 1 tablespoon oil, soy sauce, 2 and ½ tablespoons water, Worcestershire sauce and allspice, toss, introduce in the oven and bake at 375 degrees F for 45 minutes.
2. Heat up a pan with 2 tablespoons oil over medium heat, add the onion, stir and cook for 5 minutes.
3. Add the cabbage, stir, cook for 5 minutes more and take off the heat.
4. In a bowl, mix the vinegar with tomato paste, dill, paprika, ¼ cup water, salt and pepper, whisk well, pour over the cabbage, introduce it in the oven and bake at 375 degrees F for 30 minutes.
5. Divide the cabbage into bowls, top with baked tofu and serve.

Enjoy!

Herbed Salmon

This is a very elegant and special dish, perfect for any dinner party!

Preparation time: 10 minutes

Cooking time: 25 minutes

Servings: 4

Ingredients:

- 4 salmon fillets, boneless, pockets cut in the center
- A pinch of lemon pepper
- A pinch of salt and black pepper
- Cooking spray
- 3 tablespoons lemon juice
- 4 tablespoons mozzarella, shredded
- 2 tablespoons dill, chopped
- 2 tablespoons chives, chopped

- 2 tablespoons thyme, chopped

Method:
1. Season fish fillets with salt, pepper and lemon pepper and drizzle the lemon juice over them.
2. Arrange the fillets in a baking dish greased with cooking spray, stuff them with shredded cheese, dill, chives and thyme, introduce in the oven and bake at 400 degrees F for 25 minutes.
3. Divide between plates and serve.

Enjoy!

Finnish Beef Mix

This is so flavored and it looks so great!
Preparation time: 10 minutes
Cooking time: 7 hours
Servings: 5
Ingredients:

- 1 and ½ pounds beef, cubed

- 2 beef stock cubes
- 1 yellow onion, chopped
- 2 carrots, sliced
- 2 tablespoons flour
- 4 tablespoons butter
- 2 cups cream

Method:

1. Heat up a pan over medium high heat, add the beef mixed with the flour, stir, brown for 5 minutes and transfer to your slow cooker.
2. Add beef cubes, onion, carrots, butter and the cream, stir, cover and cook on Low for 7 hours.
3. Divide the mixture into bowls and serve.

Enjoy!

Reindeer Stew

We can bet you've never tried such a tasty dish!

Preparation time: 10 minutes
Cooking time: 25 minutes
Servings: 4
Ingredients:

- ½ pound reindeer meat, sliced
- 1 yellow onion, chopped
- ¼ pound chanterelle mushrooms, sliced
- 1 and ½ tablespoons vegetable oil
- 1 cup cream
- 5 juniper berries, dried
- 5 tablespoons black currant jelly
- A pinch of salt and black pepper
- 2 tablespoons parsley, chopped
- Boiled potatoes for serving

Method:

1. Heat up a pan with the oil over medium high heat, add the onion, stir and cook for 3-4 minutes.

2. Add the meat, stir and then cook for 5 minutes more.
3. Add the mushrooms, stir and cook for 2 more minutes.
4. Add the cream, juniper berries, the jelly, salt and pepper, stir, bring to a simmer and cook over medium heat for 15 minutes.
5. Add the parsley, stir, divide between plates and serve with boiled potatoes on the side.

   Enjoy!

Stuffed Peppers

Make some delicious stuffed peppers the Finnish way!

Preparation time: 10 minutes

Cooking time: 30 minutes

Servings: 4

Ingredients:

- 4 red bell peppers, tops cut off, insides scooped out
- 2 tablespoons cheddar, grated
- ½ pound beef, ground
- 1 yellow onion, chopped
- 2 ounces white mushrooms, sliced

- 1 egg, whisked
- 1 cup crème fraiche
- A pinch of salt and black pepper
- 2 teaspoons tomato paste

Method:
1. Heat up a pan over medium heat, add the beef and brown it for 4 minutes.
2. Add the onion and the mushrooms, stir and cook for 2 minutes more.
3. Add the egg, crème fraiche, salt, pepper and tomato paste, stir well, cook for 2 minutes more and take off the heat.
4. Stuff the peppers with this mix, arrange them all in a baking dish, sprinkle the cheese all over and bake in the oven at 400 degrees F for 20 minutes.
5. Divide the peppers between plates and serve.

Enjoy!

Creamy Rutabaga Bake

It's such a rich dish! You can serve it for lunch anytime!

Preparation time: 10 minutes

Cooking time: 1 hour

Servings: 4

Ingredients:

- 6 cups rutabagas, diced
- 3 tablespoons butter
- ¾ cup half and half
- ¾ cup bread crumbs
- A pinch of salt
- A pinch of nutmeg powder

- 2 eggs, whisked

Method:
1. Put the rutabagas in a pan, add water to cover, bring to a simmer over medium heat, cook for 20 minutes, drain, mash and put in a bowl.
2. Add the eggs, bread crumbs, half of the butter, salt, nutmeg and half and half and stir well.
3. Grease a baking dish with the rest of the butter, pour and spread the rutabaga mix, introduce in the oven, bake at 350 degrees F for 45 minutes, slice and serve.

Enjoy!

Fish Dinner Mix

Who won't appreciate a great fish dish?
Preparation time: 10 minutes
Cooking time: 25 minutes
Servings: 4
Ingredients:

- 1 pound salmon fillets, boneless and cubed
- ½ teaspoon dill, dried
- 1 yellow onion, chopped
- A pinch of salt and black pepper
- 4 cups water
- 4 potatoes, cubed
- 2 cups milk
- 2 tablespoons butter
- 1 tablespoon chives, chopped

Method:

1. Put the water in a pot, add potatoes, salt, pepper, dill and the onion, stir, bring to a simmer over medium heat and cook for 20 minutes.

2. Add the milk combined with the butter and whisk.
3. Also add the salmon, toss, cook for 5 minutes more, divide into bowls and serve with the chives sprinkled on top.

Enjoy!

Roasted Salmon

This recipe is very simple and delicious!

Preparation time: 10 minutes
Cooking time: 20 minutes
Servings: 4
Ingredients:

- 2 teaspoons lemon juice
- ½ cup sour cream
- 1/3 cup yogurt
- 1/3 cup dill, chopped
- Salt and black pepper to the taste
- 3 ounces rye bread crumbs
- 4 teaspoons olive oil
- 2 scallions thinly sliced
- 4 medium salmon fillets

Method:
1. In a bowl, mix the bread crumbs with the dill, salt, pepper, scallions, yogurt and sour cream and stir well.
2. Grease a baking dish with the oil, add fish fillets, spread the dill cream all over, drizzle the lemon juice, introduce in the oven and bake at 400 degrees F for 20 minutes.
3. Divide the salmon between plates and serve.

Enjoy!

Pork and Beef Meatballs

Serve them right away! They are so good!

Preparation time: 10 minutes

Cooking time: 10 minutes

Servings: 6

Ingredients:

- 4 whole wheat bread slices, crumbled
- ½ cup whole milk
- 12 ounces ground pork meat
- 12 ounces ground beef meat

- 1 egg, whisked
- ½ cup yellow onion, chopped
- ¼ teaspoon ground allspice
- Salt and black pepper to the taste
- ¼ teaspoon nutmeg powder
- 2 tablespoons butter
- 1 tablespoon white flour
- 2 tablespoons olive oil
- 1 cup chicken stock
- 1 cup fresh cranberries
- ¼ cup heavy cream
- 1 teaspoon lemon zest, grated
- 1 tablespoon lemon juice
- 2 teaspoons sugar
- 1 teaspoon ginger, grated
- 2 tablespoons dill, chopped
- 2 tablespoons parsley, chopped

Method:

1. Put bread in a bowl, add whole milk, soak for 5 minutes, drain well and put in another bowl.
2. Add pork, beef, egg, onion, nutmeg, allspice, salt and pepper, stir well and shape medium meatballs out of this mixture.
3. Heat up a pan with half of the oil and half of the butter over medium heat, add the meatballs, cook them for 4 minutes on each side and transfer them to a plate.
4. Heat up another pan with the rest of the oil and the rest of the butter over medium heat, add the flour and whisk it well.
5. Add stock, salt, pepper and cream, stir, bring to a simmer over medium low heat, add the meatballs and cook them for 10 minutes.
6. In your food processor, mix cranberries with lemon zest, lemon juice, sugar, ginger, salt, pepper, dill and parsley and pulse well.
7. Divide the meatballs mix between plates, add the cranberry sauce on the side and serve.

Enjoy!

Tasty Beef Steaks

This is a very popular Finnish dish!

Preparation time: 10 minutes

Cooking time: 10 minutes

Servings: 4

Ingredients:

- 4 medium sirloin steaks
- Salt and black pepper to the taste
- 1 tablespoon vegetable oil
- 1 tablespoon butter, soft
- 8 cherry tomatoes, halved

- A small handful tarragon, chopped

Method:
1. Heat up a pan with the oil and the butter over medium high heat, add steaks, cook them for 2 minutes on each side and transfer to your preheated grill over medium high heat.
2. Cook the steaks for 2 more minutes on each side, divide them between plates and season with salt and pepper.
3. Heat up the pan with the oil and the butter over medium high heat, add the tomatoes and the tarragon, toss, cook for 5-6 minutes, add next to the steaks and serve.

Enjoy!

Flavored Chicken Mix

The taste is simply excellent!
Preparation time: 10 minutes
Cooking time: 1 hour
Servings: 2
Ingredients:
- 3 ounces morels, sliced
- 2 tablespoons white flour
- 2 tablespoons butter
- Salt and black pepper to the taste
- 2 chicken breasts, skinless and boneless
- 1 teaspoon tarragon, minced

- 1 and ¼ cups chicken stock
- 4 shallots, diced
- 4 tablespoons heavy cream
- 1 tablespoon dry sherry
- 1 tablespoon lemon juice

Method:

1. In a bowl, mix flour with salt and pepper, stir and dredge the chicken in this mix.
2. Heat up a pan with 1 tablespoon butter over medium high heat, add chicken and brown for 4 minutes on each side.
3. Transfer chicken pieces in a baking dish, add half of the chicken stock, introduce in the oven at 300 degrees F and bake for 40 minutes.
4. Heat up another pan with 1 tablespoon butter over medium high heat, add shallots and morels, stir and cook for 4 minutes.
5. Add the rest of the chicken stock, stir, bring to a simmer and cook for 10-15 minutes.
6. Add lemon juice, cream and the sherry stir and cook for 10 more minutes.
7. Slice chicken breasts, divide between plates, add the morels mixture on the side and serve with tarragon sprinkled on top.

Enjoy!

Trout and Spinach

It's so fantastic and easy to make! You'll see!

Preparation time: 10 minutes

Cooking time: 30 minutes

Servings: 4

Ingredients:

- 1 and ¼ pounds trout fillets, boneless
- Salt and black pepper to the taste
- 1 small yellow onion, chopped
- 6 ounces mushrooms sliced
- 2 tablespoons vegetable oil
- 9 ounces spinach, torn

- 2 garlic cloves, minced
- 3 tablespoons pine nuts

For the sauce:

- ¾ cup fish stock
- ¾ cup whipping cream
- ¾ cup Parmesan, grated
- 4 tablespoons white wine

Method:

1. Put the stock in a pot, heat up over medium heat, add the cream and the wine, stir and simmer for 15 minutes.
2. Take this off the heat, add the Parmesan, whisk well and cool down a few minutes.
3. Heat up another pan with the vegetable oil over medium high heat, add mushrooms and onions, stir and cook for 3-4 minutes.
4. Add garlic, spinach, salt and pepper, cook for 2 minutes and spread into a baking dish.
5. Add the fish fillets, season them with salt and pepper, spread the creamy sauce you've prepared, introduce in the oven and bake at 425 degrees F for 15 minutes.
6. Divide the fish, the spinach and the sauce between plates and serve.

1. Enjoy!

Fish Pudding

It's one of the best fish dishes you'll ever make!

Preparation time: 10 minutes

Cooking time: 1 hour and 10 minutes

Servings: 6

Ingredients:

- 1 yellow onion, chopped
- 2 pounds potatoes, cubed
- 1 tablespoon butter
- 1 pound salmon fillets, boneless and cubed
- 3 eggs
- 2 ounces dill+ 1 tablespoon, chopped
- 1 and ¼ cups milk
- ½ cup whipping cream
- Salt and white pepper to the taste
- Lemon wedges for serving

Method:

1. Put potatoes in a pot, add water to cover, boil over medium high

heat for 20 minutes, drain and put in a bowl.
2. Heat up a pan with the butter over medium heat, add onion and sauté for 4 minutes.
3. Grease a baking dish with some butter, spread half of potatoes and half of the onions on the bottom, also add half of the salmon and 1 ounce dill.
4. Repeat with the rest potatoes, onions, salmon and dill.
5. In a bowl, mix eggs with salt, pepper, cream and milk, whisk, pour over the salmon pudding and bake at 400 degrees F for 45 minutes.
6. Divide the pudding between plates, sprinkle 1 tablespoon dill all over and serve with lemon wedges on the side.

Enjoy!

Smoked Mackerel Mix

It's so healthy and delicious!

Preparation time: 10 minutes
Cooking time: 0 minutes
Servings: 8
Ingredients:

- 7 ounces smoked mackerel fillets skinless and flaked
- Juice of ½ lemon
- Zest of ½ lemon, grated
- 4 tablespoons crème fraiche
- A pinch of black pepper
- A small bunch of chives, chopped
- A small handful dill, chopped
- 1 chicory head, shredded

Method:

1. In a bowl, mix the mackerel with lemon juice, lemon zest, crème fraiche, chives, black pepper, dill and chicory, toss, divide between plates and serve.

Enjoy!

Smoked Salmon Bowls

This is one traditional Finnish idea you simply have to try!

Preparation time: 5 minutes

Cooking time: 0 minutes

Servings: 8

Ingredients:

- 3 tablespoons white horseradish cream
- 1 cup heavy cream
- 2 teaspoons mustard
- 1 pound smoked salmon, boneless, skinless and flaked
- ¼ teaspoon black pepper

Method:

1. In a bowl, combine the horseradish cream with the heavy cream, mustard, salmon and black pepper, toss, divide into small bowls and serve.

Enjoy!

Ceviche

Prepare this special and super easy dish right away!

Preparation time: 10 minutes
Cooking time: 1 hour
Servings: 2
Ingredients:

- 1 grapefruit, cubed
- 1 avocado, pitted, peeled and chopped
- 4 ounces smoked salmon, boneless, skinless and cut into small pieces
- 1 red onion, chopped

Method:

1. In a bowl, mix the grapefruit with the avocado, salmon and onion, toss, divide between plates and serve for dinner.

Enjoy!

Finnish Dessert Recipes

Every delicious and magical meal must end with a tasty and sweet dessert! We thought you could all enjoy some of the best Finnish desserts! Learn to make them all and make everyone happy!

Simple Rice Fritters

These are pretty simple to make at home!

Preparation time: 10 minutes

Cooking time: 6 minutes

Servings: 4

Ingredients:

- 1 cup white rice, cooked
- 2 eggs, whisked
- 2 tablespoons raisins
- ¼ teaspoon lemon zest, grated
- 2 tablespoons almonds, chopped
- 3 tablespoons white flour
- 4 tablespoons butter, melted
- 1 tablespoon sugar

Method:

1. In a bowl, mix the rice with eggs, raisins, lemon zest, almonds, sugar and flour, stir well and make small cakes out of this mix.

2. Heat up a pan with the butter over medium high heat, add the cakes, cook them for 3 minutes on each side and serve.

   Enjoy!

Finnish Cookies

These cookies are so delicious! We love them!

Preparation time: 10 minutes
Cooking time: 10 minutes
Servings: 4
Ingredients:

- 1 cup soft butter
- ½ cup sugar
- 1 teaspoon almond extract
- 3 cups flour
- 3 eggs, whisked
- 1 and ½ cups almonds, chopped

Method:

1. In a bowl, combine the butter with the sugar, eggs, almond

extract, flour and almonds, stir well and shape medium sticks out of this mix.
2. Arrange the cookies on a lined baking sheet, introduce in the oven and bake at 350 degrees F for 10 minutes.
3. Serve the cookies cold.

Enjoy!

Tasty Round Cookies

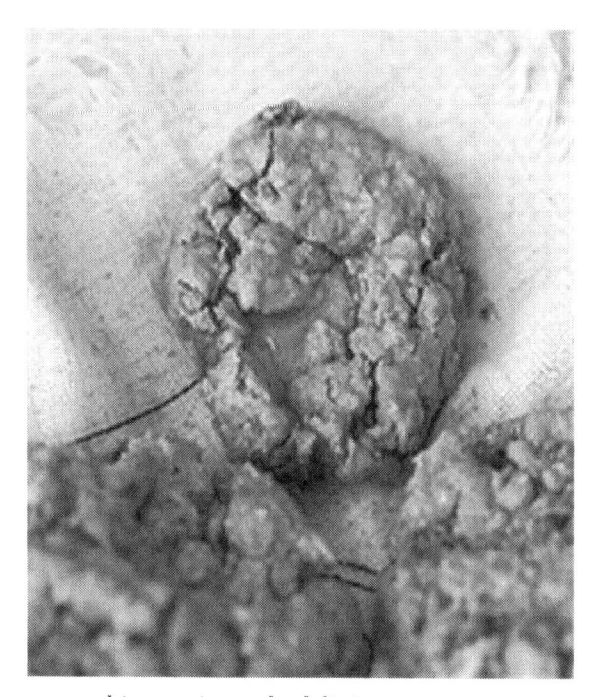

These cardamom cookies are insanely delicious!

Preparation time: 10 minutes

Cooking time: 12 minutes

Servings: 4

Ingredients:

- 1 cup flour
- 1 teaspoon cinnamon powder
- ¼ teaspoon baking soda
- 1 teaspoon cardamom powder
- 1 egg
- ½ cup butter, melted
- ¾ cup sugar

Method:

1. In a bowl, mix the flour with the cinnamon, baking soda, cardamom, egg, sugar and butter and stir well.

2. Drop spoonfuls out of this mix on a lined baking sheet, flatten into rounds, introduce in the oven and bake at 350 degrees F for 12 minutes.
3. Serve them warm.

Enjoy!

Great Cranberry Cream

The taste is so fresh!

Preparation time: 10 minutes
Cooking time: 15 minutes
Servings: 4
Ingredients:

- 2 cups cranberries
- 1 cup sugar
- 1 and ½ cups water
- 1/3 cup farina

Method:

1. Put the water in a pot, bring to a simmer over medium heat, add the cranberries, boil for 5 minutes and mash everything a bit.
2. Add the sugar and the farina, whisk, cook for 10 minutes, divide into bowls and serve.

Enjoy!

Blueberry Pie

This looks incredible and it tastes so amazing!

Preparation time: 10 minutes
Cooking time: 30 minutes
Servings: 5
Ingredients:

- 1 cup almond milk
- 2 teaspoons dry yeast
- 2/3 cup sugar

- 1 egg
- 3 cups flour
- 1/3 cup butter, melted
- 4 cups blueberries
- 3 tablespoons almond flour

Method:

1. In a bowl, combine the milk with the yeast, sugar, egg, white flour and butter and stir well.
2. In another bowl, mix the blueberries with the almond flour and toss.
3. Pour the batter into a pie pan, spread the blueberries all over and bake in the oven at 350 degrees F for 30 minutes.
4. Slice the pie and serve it cold.

Enjoy!

Plums Stew

It's going to be ready in just a few minutes!
Preparation time: 10 minutes
Cooking time: 15 minutes
Servings: 4
Ingredients:

- 1 pound plums, stones removed
- 1 cup water
- ½ cup sugar
- 5 cardamom pods, crushed

Method:
1. Put the water in a pot, bring to a simmer over medium heat, add plums, sugar and cardamom, stir, cook for 15 minutes, divide into bowls and serve cold.

Enjoy!

Rhubarb Puddings

This is one dessert your kids will adore!

Preparation time: 10 minutes
Cooking time: 40 minutes
Servings: 4
Ingredients:

- 5 tablespoons sugar
- 12 ounces rhubarb, chopped
- Zest of 1 orange, grated
- Juice of 1 orange
- 2 tablespoons water
- 1 and ¼ cups heavy cream
- ½ cup milk
- ¼ cup sugar
- 1 teaspoon vanilla extract
- 2 gelatin sheets

Method:

1. In a bowl, mix the rhubarb with orange zest, orange juice, 5 tablespoons sugar and 2 tablespoons water, toss, spread into a baking dish, bake at 350 degrees F for 30 minutes and cool down.
2. Heat up the milk in a pot over medium heat, add the heavy cream, ¼ cup sugar and vanilla extract, stir, bring to a simmer and take off the heat.
3. Put gelatin in a bowl, add cold water to cover, soak for 5 minutes, drain, add over the cream mixture and whisk well.
4. Strain this into 4 ramekins and keep in the fridge for 3 hours.
5. Heat up the rhubarb in the microwave for a few seconds.
6. Take ramekins out of the fridge, put the bases in hot water for 30 seconds, then tip them out between plates, top each with the rhubarb mix and serve.

Enjoy!

Red Currant Smoothie

This is perfect after an amazing meal!

Preparation time: 10 minutes
Cooking time: 0 minutes
Servings: 2
Ingredients:

- 1 banana, peeled
- 8 ounces redcurrants, trimmed
- 1 cup plain yogurt
- 5 tablespoons cranberry syrup
- A drizzle of honey

Method:

1. In a blender, mix the banana with the red currants, yogurt and cranberry syrup, pulse well, divide into small glasses, drizzle the honey on top and serve.

    Enjoy!

Rich Rice Pudding

It will hypnotize you!

Preparation time: 10 minutes
Cooking time: 1 hour
Servings: 8
Ingredients:

- 3 cups milk
- 1 cup rice cooked
- 3 eggs, whisked
- ¼ cup butter, melted
- ½ cup sugar

- 1 teaspoon cinnamon powder
- ½ cup almonds, sliced

Method:

1. In a bowl, mix cooked rice with eggs, sugar, milk and melted butter, stir well, pour into a baking dish, sprinkle cinnamon and almonds on top, introduce in the oven at 350 degrees F and bake everything for 1 hour.
2. Transfer to dessert bowls and serve.

    Enjoy!

Apple Pie

The flavor is great and the taste is even better!

Preparation time: 10 minutes

Cooking time: 25 minutes

Servings: 4

Ingredients:

- 2 and ½ pounds apples, cored, peeled and sliced
- 1 cup sugar

- 1 tablespoon cinnamon powder
- 1 cup bread crumbs
- 1/3 cup butter

For serving:

- 1 and ¼ cups whipping cream
- 3 egg yolks.
- 7 tablespoons sugar

Method:

1. In a bowl, mix apples with cinnamon, bread crumbs and sugar, toss, arrange this into a baking dish, spread 1/3 cup butter on top and bake in the oven at 390 degrees F for 25 minutes.
2. Put 1 cup whipping cream in a pot, heat up over medium heat, add 7 tablespoons sugar, stir well and bring to a simmer.
3. In a bowl, mix the egg yolks with some of the cream mix, whisk, pour into the pot, stir well and take off the heat.
4. Add the rest of the whipping cream and whisk well again.
5. Divide the pie between plates, top each serving with the cream mixture and serve.

Enjoy!

Conclusion

This Finnish recipe collection is truly spectacular! You've just discovered the best and most amazing Finnish recipes! You learned how to prepare some incredible Finnish breakfasts, salads, soups, main dishes and of course, some delightful desserts. All you need is to get your hands on a copy of this magnificent cooking journal and to bring some of the Finnish flavors into your homes. The traditional Finnish cuisine is here and it will conquer you for good!

Start your culinary journey through Finnish delights right now and enjoy the best time!

Have fun and cooking original and rich Finnish dishes!

Author's Afterthoughts

Thank you for reading my book. Your feedback is important to us.

Made in the USA
Middletown, DE
06 August 2023